DANGEROUS JOBS

LOGGING

G.L. CRONIN

Rourke Educational Media
A Division of Carson Dellosa Education
rourkeeducationalmedia.com

ROURKE'S **SCHOOL to HOME** CONNECTIONS

BEFORE AND DURING READING ACTIVITIES

Before Reading: *Building Background Knowledge and Vocabulary*

Building background knowledge can help children process new information and build upon what they already know. Before reading a book, it is important to tap into what children already know about the topic. This will help them develop their vocabulary and increase their reading comprehension.

Questions and Activities to Build Background Knowledge:

1. Look at the front cover of the book and read the title. What do you think this book will be about?
2. What do you already know about this topic?
3. Take a book walk and skim the pages. Look at the table of contents, photographs, captions, and bold words. Did these text features give you any information or predictions about what you will read in this book?

Vocabulary: *Vocabulary Is Key to Reading Comprehension*

Use the following directions to prompt a conversation about each word.

- Read the vocabulary words.
- What comes to mind when you see each word?
- What do you think each word means?

Vocabulary Words:

- *acres*
- *harvest*
- *pulp*
- *remote*
- *steep*
- *timber*

During Reading: *Reading for Meaning and Understanding*

To achieve deep comprehension of a book, children are encouraged to use close reading strategies. During reading, it is important to have children stop and make connections. These connections result in deeper analysis and understanding of a book.

Close Reading a Text

During reading, have children stop and talk about the following:

- Any confusing parts
- Any unknown words
- Text to text, text to self, text to world connections
- The main idea in each chapter or heading

Encourage children to use context clues to determine the meaning of any unknown words. These strategies will help children learn to analyze the text more thoroughly as they read.

When you are finished reading this book, turn to the next-to-last page for **After Reading Questions** and an **Activity**.

Table of Contents

The Logging Life

A logger yells, “Timber!” A tree falls. Loggers know to stay clear.

Logging is the most dangerous job in America. About 136 loggers of every 100,000 die on the job each year.

Second Place

Logging is 39 times more dangerous than most jobs. The second most dangerous job in America is working on a fishing boat. But logging is twice as risky.

How do loggers get hurt? Trees and branches fall. Equipment can tumble down **steep** mountains.

steep (steep): very high

A logger's workday begins before dawn. Loggers go to **remote** forests. They work outside in rain, snow, wind, and cold.

Where Are They?

GPS (Global Positioning System) keeps track of loggers. If there is an emergency, help can find them.

remote (ri-MOHT): far away from towns and cities

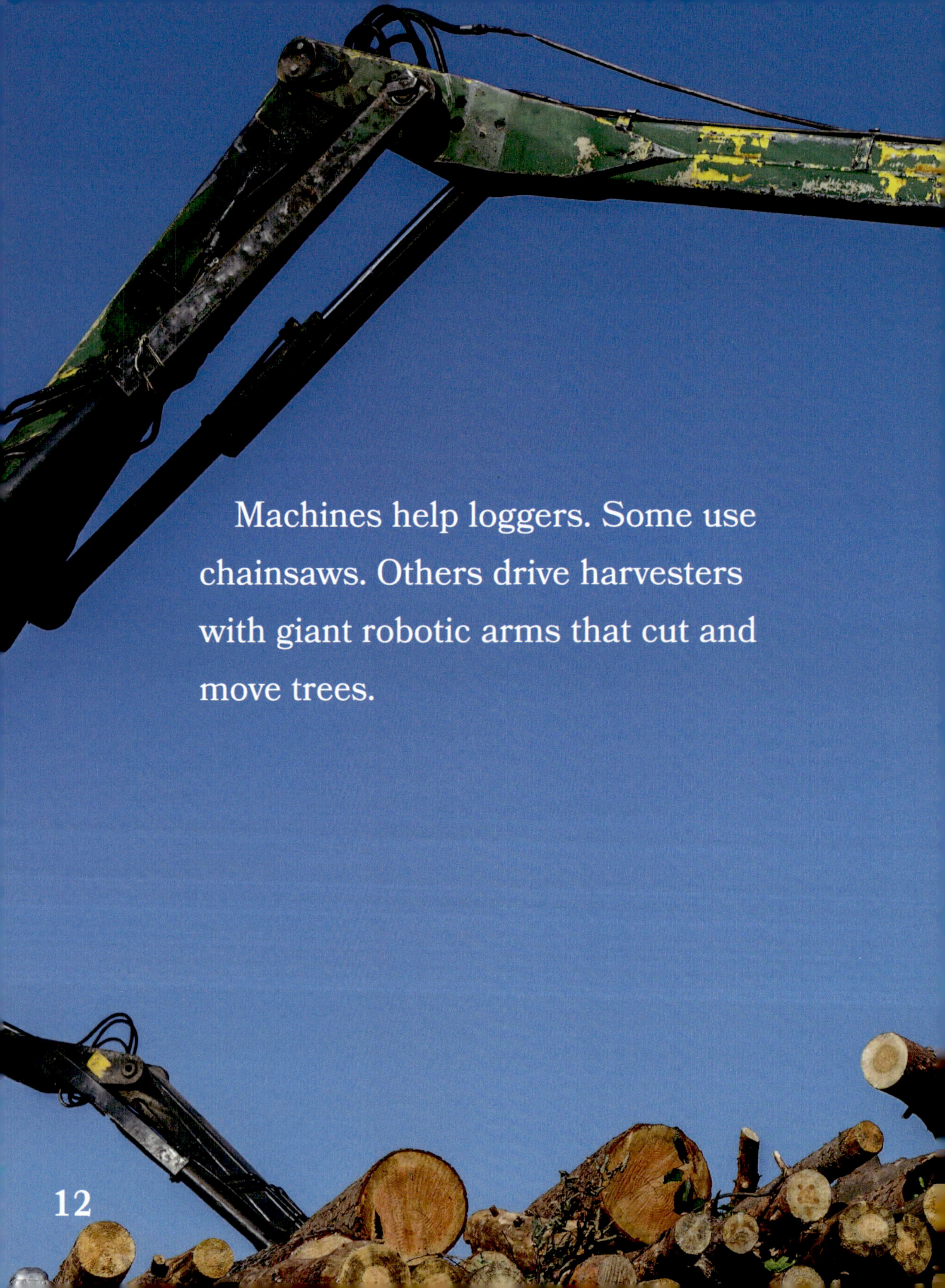

Machines help loggers. Some use chainsaws. Others drive harvesters with giant robotic arms that cut and move trees.

Warning!

A chainsaw's loud noise can hurt hearing. Sharp blades are dangerous.

Loggers harvest thousands of **acres** of forest each year. For selective logging, only certain trees are cut. In clear-cutting, all the trees in an area are removed.

acres (AY-kurs): areas that are each equal to 43,560 square feet (4,047 square meters)

Fearless Fellers

A feller's job is to bring down trees. Fellers must keep safety in mind. A tree can weigh 50 tons (45 metric tons). That's heavier than five elephants!

Falling Zone

Stand one-and-a-half tree lengths back. This rule saves fellers' lives.

Fellers walk through the woods. They make a plan for which trees to **harvest**. They look for safe ways to escape in case there is an accident.

harvest (HAHR-vist): to gather crops or trees

Fellers with chainsaws make cuts at the top, bottom, and back. They make the felling cut last. This helps control where the tree will fall.

Suit Up!

Loggers wear personal protective equipment (PPE). They protect their faces, feet, and hands.

Dead trees are called snags. Snags can hurt or kill loggers when they fall and roll. Fellers make sure to remove them.

Silent Killers

Snags wobble. Dead branches break loose. A "struck-by" happens when a worker gets hit.

Brave Buckers

Buckers get **timber** ready to sell. They remove branches. They cut trees into logs.

timber (TIM-bur): cut trees used for building

Skidding is removing logs from the cutting site. A skidder drags logs across the forest floor to a road. The timber gets loaded onto trucks.

Loggers brave danger so we have the wood we need. Some will be used in buildings and furniture. Some will become **pulp** for paper.

pulp (puhlp): the soft, juicy mixture of wood and water used to make paper

Memory Game

Look at the pictures. What do you remember reading on the pages where each image appeared?

Index

After Reading Questions

1. What is the falling zone?
2. How do machines help loggers?
3. What job duties do fellers complete?
4. What are dead trees called, and why do they endanger loggers?
5. Why do loggers wear personal protective equipment (PPE) and how does this equipment keep them safe?

Activity

Do some research about how logging has changed over time. Then, write a story in which a logger time-travels from 200 years ago, to the present, and into the future.

About the Author

G.L. Cronin enjoys researching intriguing topics. She especially likes learning about anything involving nature. In addition to writing, she works as a middle school librarian.

www.rourkeeducationalmedia.com

PHOTO CREDITS: Cover (top), page 1 (top): ©vm; cover (bottom), page 1 (bottom): ©abadonian; pages 4-5, 24-25, 30: ©simonkr; pages 6-7: ©stocknshares; pages 8-9, 30: ©rikukankano.net; pages 10-11: ©vicsa; pages 12-13, 30: ©taseffski; pages 14-15: ©halbergman; pages 16-17: ©JosefMohyla; pages 18-19, 30: ©Pojbic; pages 20-21: ©MartinFredy; pages 22-23: ©ulimi; pages 26-27, 30: ©Cucu Remus; pages 28-29: ©AndreiStaneSCU; pages 30-31©Main_sail

Edited by: Kim Thompson
Cover and interior design by: Rhea Magaro-Wallace

Library of Congress PCN Data

Logging / G.L. Cronin
(Dangerous Jobs)
ISBN 978-1-73161-510-7 (hard cover)
ISBN 978-1-73161-317-2 (soft cover)
ISBN 978-1-73161-615-9 (e-Book)
ISBN 978-1-73161-720-0 (ePub)
Library of Congress Control Number: 2019932155

Rourke Educational Media
Printed in the United States of America,
North Mankato, Minnesota